P9-CQE-589

Warfighting

THE
UNITED STATES
MARINE CORPS

CURRENCY
DOUBLEDAY

New York   London   Toronto   Sydney   Auckland

A CURRENCY PAPERBACK
PUBLISHED BY DOUBLEDAY

a division of Bantam Doubleday Dell Publishing Group, Inc.
1540 Broadway, New York, New York 10036

CURRENCY and DOUBLEDAY are trademarks of Doubleday,
a division of Bantam Doubleday Dell Publishing Group, Inc.

Warfighting was originally published in hardcover by
Currency Doubleday in 1994.

The Library of Congress has cataloged the Currency hardcover edition as
follows:
Warfighting/the United States Marine Corps. — 1st ed.
p.   cm.
"A Currency book."
Originally published: Washington, D.C.: U.S. Marine Corps, 1989.
Includes bibliographical references.
1. United States. Marine Corps—Handbooks, manuals, etc.
2. Military doctrine—United States—Handbooks, manuals, etc.
3. Maneuver warfare—Handbooks, manuals, etc.   I. United States
Marine Corps.
[VE153.W37   1994]

355'.002'02—dc20   94-1651
                                                                   CIP

13 15 17 19 20 18 16 14 12

Contents

A Philosophy of Action for All

In 1989 U.S. Marine Corps Commandant General A. M. Gray distributed a remarkable 77-page document to every officer in the Corps. Authentically written and brilliantly articulate, *Warfighting*, the official doctrine of the U.S. Marine Corps, calls to mind other classics of strategy such as Sun Tzu's *The Art of War*, Carl von Clausewitz's *On War*, and Miyamoto Musashi's *The Book of Five Rings*.

Like those books, which were written as philosophical guides for military officers, *Warfighting* can be put to use by people in all fields, in virtually every endeavor. Mark B. Fuller, cofounder and CEO of Michael Porter's strategic consulting firm, Monitor Company, put it succinctly: "Replace the word 'combat' with competition, 'officer' with manager, 'soldier' with front-line-worker, 'enemy' with rival, and *Warfighting* becomes a remarkably trenchant management handbook."[1] What competitive edge do Marines bring to tough business situations? To find out, the editors of Currency Doubleday asked this question of a group of former Marines:

- F. LEE BAILEY, attorney
- ED MCMAHON, TV personality
- DONALD REGAN, former chairman of Merrill Lynch and White House Chief of Staff under President Ronald Reagan
- TOM MONAGHAN, CEO of Domino's Pizza
- JAMES A. BAKER III, 61st Secretary of State and 67th Secretary of the Treasury.

These men, who have lived the ideas this book sets forth, emphasize the Marine Corps' skills of preparedness, flexibility, boldness, and moral courage. Here they are in their own words:

F. LEE BAILEY: The remarkable thing about *Warfighting* is that it is laid out so simply, like a primer. Even if you don't intend to rush out and start your own military branch or commence warfighting, the analogies—the tactics, feints, flanks, attacks—all apply in other walks of life.

I use my military training every day. Trials are miniwars. People are under stress: some are cowards, some brave. Lives are often on the line. In the courtroom, circumstances change from moment to moment, and so do legal strategies. Flexibility is essential. A bad lawyer walks in with a list of questions. A good one walks in with a head stuffed full of facts. He's ready and he wins. There are strategic questions as well. How do I go in? Do I commit at the beginning, or hang back and see how the affray is going?

A lawyer must use any legitimate weapon to achieve his objective. Deception and intimidation—under the tight collar of professional ethics—are tools of lawyers as well as soldiers. I will keep a prosecutor guessing. I will use everything I can to get someone to say what I need them to say. In one instance, I wanted to encourage a powerful executive to settle out of court. I went out and memorized thirty speeches the man had made and fed his own words back to him, adding here, deleting there, until finally I had him agreeing to some very damaging things. He settled. If I had not been prepared, he'd have won. Preparation that is thorough enough to achieve the state that *Warfighting* calls "readiness" is critical in court as well as in battle. When I asked my friend and mentor, Edward Bennett Williams, how to pull a rabbit out of a hat in court, he said, "Bring fifty rabbits and fifty hats."

ED MCMAHON: I have learned two important lessons from my association with the Marine Corps: always be on time and always be ready to do what is required when you get there. "Be ready" is a key component in the life of a Marine. In my business that includes an infinite amount of preparation: knowing one's lines, having the correct wardrobe, being ready in every way to tackle the job assigned. Being a good Marine transfers easily to being successful in your chosen field.

DONALD REGAN: In *Warfighting* General Gray says: "Whoever can make and implement his decisions consistently faster gains a tremendous, often decisive advantage."[2] This can mean launching a surprise attack or it can mean getting a new product to market *years* before the competition, as was the case with Merrill Lynch's Cash Management Account [CMA]. We invented CMA—an account that combines checking, securities trading, and charge card—in the seventies when I was chairman. Half my staff thought this was the best idea they'd ever heard, the other half thought it was bound to be illegal. I decided to go ahead, state by state, and set the precedent for a whole new way of banking. By 1980, when asked what the future held for banking, a well-respected competitor of ours said, "Look at Merrill Lynch, that's the future."

General Gray says, "We must have the moral courage necessary to make bold decisions and accept the necessary degree of risk when the natural inclination is to choose a less ambitious tack, for 'in audacity and obstinacy will be found safety.'"[3] This was true in the Reagan White House, when we took "a riverboat gamble" and cut taxes. Everyone cried out that this drastic measure would lead to ruin. But what it led to was the prosperity of the eighties. Now more than ever, business people need the Marine advantage—confidence, training, maneuverability, speed, and boldness. Today's global competitions demand quick decision making and bold implementation. Those that can't rise to this standard will surely be left at the starting gate.

TOM MONAGHAN: I didn't go to college. The Marine Corps taught me to be a leader. Part of being a Marine is understanding that at any moment you may be called upon to lead. You must always be prepared to assume complete responsibility. When words get coarse and tempers flare, it's good to have the kind of self-confidence instilled by the Marines. A Marine is never intimidated. Once when I was a young Marine, I was confronted by an ex-Golden Glove boxer. I stood up to him—and took a beating as you would expect. But that man treated me with respect from then on. The same is true in business: people respect people who stand up for themselves. There is no better school of confidence than the U.S. Marine Corps and there is no one better qualified to present the Marine Corps doctrine than General (ret.) A. M. Gray. He's every bit the caliber of Chesty Puller, the most decorated Marine in history.

JAMES A. BAKER III: I joined the Corps when I graduated from college in 1952, during a time when we were concerned with the Red Army in Europe, Red China in Asia, and a bloody conflict on the Korean Peninsula. The world was very different then, but my experience in the Corps transcended that particular time, maturing me personally and professionally and preparing me for work in public service and the private sector.

The two years I spent in the Marine Corps were an important turning point in my life. My military service showed me the value of love of God and country, the importance of duty, and the sanctity of honor. It taught me the value of the security that so many Americans, then as now, take for granted. And it gave me a sense of the cost—the human cost—of defending that security.

Little did I realize in 1952 that I would later be faced so personally with the cost of American security as I was in January 1991, when I concluded a nonproductive six-hour meeting with Iraqi Foreign Minister Tariq Aziz, knowing then for sure that American troops would soon be at war. It was a solemn moment for me, but also one of extraordinary pride—pride in the courageous young soldiers on the Saudi sands and the Gulf waters, pride in the excellence of our military services, and pride in the unwavering loyalty of the American people.

In a way, that moment in Geneva concluded my education as a citizen and a man that had begun for me as an officer candidate in Quantico nearly forty years before. As I left the conference room, I realized fully how high the price of freedom is. And I also understood just how much we all owe to those Americans who selflessly pay that price.

* * *

Reading this book will not substitute in depth and intensity for the experience of serving in the Marine Corps, but there are powerful lessons here to guide and sustain us in every confrontation, whether of a personal or business nature. In times that call for defiance and boldness there is no better role model for the warrior hidden in each of us than the one described in these pages.

This letter was written for and printed as the Foreword to the U.S. Government Printing Office edition of Warfighting.

DEPARTMENT OF THE NAVY
Headquarters United States Marine Corps
Washington, D.C.   20380-0001

6 March 1989

FOREWORD

This book describes my philosophy on warfighting. It is the Marine Corps' doctrine and, as such, provides the authoritative basis for how we fight and how we prepare to fight.

By design, this is a small book and easy to read. It is not intended as a reference manual, but is designed to be read from cover to cover. There is a natural progression to its four chapters. Chapter 1 describes our understanding of the characteristics, problems, and demands of war. Chapter 2 derives a theory about war based on that understanding. This theory in turn provides the foundation for how we prepare for war and how we wage war, chapters 3 and 4 respectively.

You will notice that this book does not contain specific techniques and procedures for conduct. Rather, it provides broad guidance in the form of concepts and values. It requires judgment in application.

I expect every officer to read—and reread—this book, understand it, and take its message to heart. The thoughts contained here represent not just guidance for actions in combat, but a way of thinking in general. This manual thus describes a philosophy for action which, in war and in peace, in the field and in the rear, dictates our approach to duty.

A. M. GRAY
General, U.S. Marine Corps
Commandant of the Marine Corps

DISTRIBUTION: TJE

CHAPTER 1

The Nature of War

"*Everything in war is simple, but the simplest thing is difficult. The difficulties accumulate and end by producing a kind of friction that is inconceivable unless one has experienced war.*"[1]

—Carl von Clausewitz

"*In war the chief incalculable is the human will.*"[2]

—B. H. Liddell Hart

"*Positions are seldom lost because they have been destroyed, but almost invariably because the leader has decided in his own mind that the position cannot be held.*"[3]

—A. A. Vandegrift

To understand the Marine Corps' philosophy of warfighting, we first need an appreciation for the nature of war itself—its moral and physical characteristics and demands.[4] A common view among Marines of the nature of war is a necessary base for the development of a cohesive doctrine.

WAR DEFINED

War is a state of hostilities that exists between or among nations, characterized by the use of military force. The essence of war is a violent clash between two hostile, independent, and irreconcilable wills, each trying to impose itself on the other.

Thus, the object of war is to impose our will on our enemy. The means to that end is the organized application or threat of violence by military force.

When significant disagreements cannot be settled through peaceful means, such as diplomacy, nations resort to war. Nations not at war with one another can be said to be at peace. However, absolute war and peace rarely exist in practice. Rather, they are extremes between which exist the relations among most nations. The need to resort to military force of some kind may arise at any point within these extremes, even during periods of relative peace. Thus, for our purposes war may range from intense clashes between large military forces—backed by an official declaration of war—to covert hostilities which barely reach the threshold of violence.[5]

FRICTION

So portrayed, war appears a simple enterprise. But in practice, because of the countless factors that impinge on it, the conduct of war becomes extremely difficult. These factors collectively have been called *friction*, which Clausewitz described as "the force that makes the apparently easy so difficult."[6] Friction is the force that resists all action. It makes the simple difficult and the difficult seemingly impossible.

The very essence of war as a clash between opposed wills creates friction. It is critical to keep in mind that the enemy is not an inanimate object but an independent and animate force. The enemy seeks to resist our will and impose his own will on us. It is the dynamic interplay between his will and ours that makes war difficult and complex. In this environment, friction abounds.

Friction may be mental, as in indecision over a course of action. Or it may be physical, as in effective enemy fire or a terrain obstacle that must be overcome. Friction may be external, imposed by enemy action, the terrain, weather, or mere chance. Or friction may be self-induced, caused by such factors as lack of a clearly defined goal, lack of coordination, unclear or complicated plans, complex task organizations or command relationships, or complicated communication systems. Whatever form it takes, because war is a human enterprise, friction will always have a psychological as well as a physical impact.

While we should attempt to minimize self-induced friction, the greater requirement is *to fight effectively within the medium of friction*. The means to overcome friction is the will; we prevail over friction through persistent strength of mind and spirit. While striving to overcome the effects of friction ourselves, we must attempt at the same time to raise our enemy's friction to a level that destroys his ability to fight.

We can readily identify countless examples of friction, but until we have experienced it ourselves, we cannot hope to appreciate it fully. Only through experience can we come to appreciate the force of will necessary to overcome friction and to develop a realistic appreciation for what is possible in war and what is not. While training should attempt to approximate the conditions of war, we must realize it can never fully duplicate the level of friction of real combat.

Uncertainty

The next attribute of the environment of war is uncertainty. We might argue that uncertainty is just one of many sources of friction, but because it is such a pervasive trait of war we will treat it singly.

All actions in war take place in an atmosphere of uncertainty—the *fog of war*. Uncertainty pervades battle in the form of unknowns about the enemy, about the environment, and even about the friendly situation. While we try to reduce these unknowns by gathering information, we must realize we cannot eliminate them. The very nature of war makes absolute certainty impossible; all actions in war will be based on incomplete, inaccurate, or even contradictory information.

At best, we can hope to determine probabilities. This implies a certain standard of military judgment: what is probable and what is not? Through this judgment of probability we make an estimate of our enemy's designs and act accordingly. But, having said this, we also realize that it is precisely those actions which fall outside the realm of probability that often have the greatest impact on the outcome of war.

We must learn to fight in an environment of uncertainty, which we can do by developing simple, flexible plans; planning for contingencies; developing standing operating procedures; and fostering initiative among subordinates.

By its nature, uncertainty invariably involves the estimation and acceptance of risk. Risk is inherent in war and is involved in every mission. Risk is also related to gain; normally, greater potential gain requires greater risk. Further, risk is equally common to action and inaction. The practice of concentrating combat power at the focus of effort necessitates the willingness to accept prudent risk. However, we should clearly understand that the acceptance of risk does not equate to the imprudent willingness to gamble the entire likelihood of success on a single improbable event.

Part of risk is the ungovernable element of chance.

The element of chance is a universal characteristic of war and a continuous source of friction. Chance consists of turns of events that cannot reasonably be foreseen and over which we and our enemy have no control. The uncontrollable *potential* for chance alone creates psychological friction. We should remember that chance favors neither belligerent exclusively. Consequently, we must view chance not only as a threat but also as an opportunity, which we must be ever ready to exploit.

FLUIDITY

Like friction and uncertainty, fluidity is an integral attribute of the nature of war. Each episode in war is the temporary result of a unique combination of circumstances, requiring an original solution. But no episode can be viewed in isolation. Rather, each merges with those that precede and follow it—shaped by the former and shaping the conditions of the latter—creating a continuous, fluctuating fabric of activity replete with fleeting opportunities and unforeseen events. Success depends in large part on the ability to adapt to a constantly changing situation.

It is physically impossible to sustain a high tempo of activity indefinitely, although clearly there will be times when it is advantageous to push men and equipment to the limit. Thus, the tempo of war will fluctuate—from periods of intense activity to periods in which activity is limited to information gathering, replenishment, or redeployment. Darkness and weather can influence the tempo of war but need not halt it. A competitive rhythm will develop between the opposing wills, with each belligerent trying to influence and exploit tempo and the continuous flow of events to suit his purposes.

DISORDER

In an environment of friction, uncertainty, and fluidity, war gravitates naturally toward disorder. Like the other attributes of the environment of war, disorder is an integral characteristic of war; we can never eliminate it. In the heat of battle, plans will go awry, instructions and information will be unclear and misinterpreted, communications will fail, and mistakes and unforeseen events will be commonplace. It is precisely this natural disorder which creates the conditions ripe for exploitation by an opportunistic will.

Each encounter in war will usually tend to grow increasingly disordered over time. As the situation changes continuously, we are forced to improvise again and again until finally our actions have little, if any, resemblance to the original scheme.

By historical standards, the modern battlefield is particularly disorderly. While past battlefields could be described by linear formations and uninterrupted linear fronts, we cannot think of today's battlefield in linear terms. The range and lethality of modern weapons has increased dispersion between units. In spite of communications technology, this dispersion strains the limits of positive control. The natural result of dispersion is unoccupied areas, gaps, and exposed flanks which can and will be exploited, blurring the distinction between front and rear and friendly- and enemy-controlled areas.

The occurrences of war will not unfold like clockwork. Thus, we cannot hope to impose precise, positive control over events. The best we can hope for is to impose a general framework of order on the disorder, to prescribe the general flow of action rather than to try to control each event.

If we are to win, we must be able to operate in a disorderly environment. In fact, we must not only be able to fight effectively in the face of disorder, we should seek to generate disorder for our opponent and use it as a weapon against him.

THE HUMAN DIMENSION

Because war is a clash between opposing human wills, the human dimension is central in war. It is the human dimension which infuses war with its intangible moral factors. War is shaped by human nature and is subject to the complexities, inconsistencies, and peculiarities which characterize human behavior. Since war is an act of violence based on irreconcilable disagreement, it will invariably inflame and be shaped by human emotions.

War is an extreme trial of moral and physical strength and stamina. Any view of the nature of war would hardly be accurate or complete without consideration of the effects of danger, fear, exhaustion, and privation on the men who must do the fighting.[7] However, these effects vary greatly from case to case. Individuals and peoples react differently to the stress of war; an act that may break the will of one enemy may only serve to stiffen the resolve of another.

No degree of technological development or scientific calculation will overcome the human dimension in war. Any doctrine which attempts to reduce warfare to ratios of forces, weapons, and equipment neglects the impact of the human will on the conduct of war and is therefore inherently false.

ware, technology, physical objectives seized, force ratios, losses of materiel or life, terrain lost or gained, prisoners or materiel captured. The moral characteristics are less tangible. (The term *moral* as used here is not restricted to ethics—although ethics are certainly included—but pertains to those forces of psychological rather than tangible nature, to include the mental aspects of war.[10]) Moral forces are difficult to grasp and impossible to quantify. We cannot easily gauge forces like national and military resolve, national or individual conscience, emotion, fear, courage, morale, leadership, or esprit. Yet moral forces exert a greater influence on the nature and outcome of war than do physical.[11] This is not to lessen the importance of physical forces, for the physical forces in war can have a significant impact on the moral. For example, the greatest effect of fires on the enemy is generally not the amount of physical destruction they cause, but the effect of that physical destruction on his moral strength.

Because the moral forces of war are difficult to come to grips with, it is tempting to exclude them from our study of war. However, any doctrine or theory of war that

Violence and Danger

War is among the greatest horrors known to mankind; it should never be romanticized. The means of war is force, applied in the form of organized violence. It is through the use of violence—or the credible threat of violence, which requires the apparent willingness to use it—that we compel our enemy to do our will. In either event, violence is an essential element of war, and its immediate result is bloodshed, destruction, and suffering. While the magnitude of violence may vary with the object and means of war, the violent essence of war will never change.[8] Any study of war that neglects this characteristic is misleading and incomplete.

Since war is a violent enterprise, danger is a fundamental characteristic of war. And since war is a human phenomenon, fear—the human reaction to danger—has a significant impact on the conduct of war. All men feel fear. Leadership must foster the courage to overcome fear, both individually and within the unit. Courage is not the absence of fear; rather, it is the strength to overcome fear.[9]

Leaders must study fear, understand it, and be prepared to cope with it. Like fear, courage takes many forms, from a stoic courage born of reasoned calculation to a fierce courage born of heightened emotion. Experience under fire generally increases courage, as can realistic training by lessening the mystique of combat. Strong leadership which earns the respect and trust of subordinates can limit the effects of fear. Leaders should develop unit cohesion and esprit and the self-confidence of individuals within the unit. In this environment a Marine's unwillingness to violate the respect and trust of his peers will overcome personal fear.

MORAL AND PHYSICAL FORCES

War is characterized by the interaction of both moral and physical forces. The physical characteristics of war are generally easily seen, understood, and measured: hard-

neglects these factors ignores the greater part of the nature of war.

THE EVOLUTION OF WAR

War is both timeless and ever changing. While the basic nature of war is constant, the means and methods we use evolve continuously. These changes may be gradual in some cases and drastic in others. Drastic changes in the nature of war are the result of developments that dramatically upset the equilibrium of war, such as the rifled bore and the railroad.

One major catalyst of change is the advancement of technology. As the physical hardware of war improves through technological development, so must the tactical, operational, and strategic usage of those means adapt to the improved capabilities—both to maximize our own capabilities and to counteract our enemy's.

We must stay abreast of this process of change, for the belligerent who first exploits a development in the art and science of war gains a significant, if not decisive, advantage. Conversely, if we are ignorant of the changing face of war, we will find ourselves unequal to its challenges.

ART AND SCIENCE OF WAR

From the discussion to this point, we can conclude that war demonstrates characteristics of both art and science. Various aspects of war, particularly its technical aspects, fall principally in the realm of science, which we will describe as the methodical application of the empirical laws of nature. The science of war includes those activities directly subject to the laws of physics, chemistry, and like disciplines; for example, the application of fires, the effects of weapons, and the rates and methods of movement and resupply. However, these are among the components of war; they do not describe the whole phenomenon. Owing to the vagaries of human behavior and the countless other intangible factors which contribute to it, there is far more to the conduct of war than can be explained by science. The science of war stops short of the need for military judgment, the impact of moral forces, the influence of chance, and other similar factors. We thus conclude that the conduct of war is ultimately an art, an activity of human creativity and intuition powered by the strength of the human will. The art of war requires the intuitive ability to grasp the essence of a unique battlefield situation, the creative ability to devise a practical solution, and the strength of purpose to execute the act.

CONCLUSION

At first glance, war seems a rather simple clash of interests. But at closer examination, it takes shape as one of the most demanding and trying of man's endeavors. Fog, friction, and chaos are its natural habitat. Each episode is the unique product of the dynamic interaction of myriad moral and physical forces. While founded on the laws of science, war demands, ultimately, the intuition and creativity of art.

CHAPTER 2

The Theory of War

"The political object is the goal, war is the means of reaching it, and the means can never be considered in isolation from their purposes."[1]

—Carl von Clausewitz

"Invincibility lies in the defense; the possibility of victory in the attack. One defends when his strength is inadequate; he attacks when it is abundant."[2]

—Sun Tzu

"Battles are won by slaughter and manoeuvre. The greater the general, the more he contributes in manoeuvre, the less he demands in slaughter."[3]

—Winston Churchill

Having arrived at a common view of the nature of war, we proceed to develop from it a theory of war. Our theory of war will in turn be the foundation for the way we prepare for and wage war.

WAR AS AN INSTRUMENT OF POLICY

War does not exist for its own sake. It is an extension of policy with military force.[4] The policy aim that is the motive for war must also be the foremost determinant for the conduct of war. The single most important thought to understand about our theory is that war *must serve policy*. As the policy aims of war may vary from resistance against aggression to complete annihilation of the enemy, so must the application of violence vary in accordance with those aims. Of course, we may also have to adjust our policy objectives to accommodate our means; we must not establish goals outside our capabilities.

When the policy motive of war is intense, such as the annihilation of an enemy, then policy and war's natural military tendency toward destruction will coincide, and the war will appear more military and less political in nature. On the other hand, the less intense the policy motive, the more the military tendency toward destruction will be at variance with that motive, and the more political and less military the war will appear.[5]

The aim in war is to achieve our will. The immediate requirement is to overcome our enemy's ability to resist us, which is a product of the physical means at his disposal and the strength of his will.[6] We must either eliminate his physical ability to resist or, short of this, we must destroy his will to resist. In military terms, this means the defeat of the enemy's fighting forces, but always in a manner and to a degree consistent with the national policy objective.

MEANS IN WAR

At the national level, war involves the use of all the elements of national power, including diplomacy, military force, economics, ideology, technology, and culture.[7] Our primary concern is with the use of *military force* as an instrument of policy. But while we will focus on the use of military force, we must not consider it in isolation from the other elements of national power. The use of military force may take any number of forms, from intense warfare with sophisticated weaponry to mere demonstrations. The principal means for the application of military force is combat—violence in the form of armed conflict between military or paramilitary forces.

THE SPECTRUM OF CONFLICT

Conflict can take a wide range of forms, constituting a spectrum which reflects the magnitude of violence involved. At one end are those conflicts of low intensity in which the application of military power is restrained and selective. The other end of the spectrum represents conflicts of high intensity, such as nuclear war. The place on the spectrum of a specific conflict depends on several factors. Among them are policy objectives, military means available, national will, and density of fighting forces or combat power on the battlefield. In general, the greater the density, the more intense the conflict. As a result, we may witness relatively intense actions within a low-intensity conflict or relatively quiet sectors or phases in an intense war.

Low-intensity conflicts are more probable than high-intensity conflicts. Many nations simply do not possess the military means to wage war at the high end of the spectrum. And, unless national survival is at stake, nations are generally unwilling to accept the risks associated with wars of high intensity. However, a conflict's intensity may change over time. Belligerents may escalate the level of violence if the original means do not achieve the desired results. Similarly, wars may actually de-escalate over time; for example, after an initial pulse of intense violence, the belligerents may continue to fight on a lesser level, unable to sustain the initial level of intensity.

The Marine Corps, as the nation's force in readiness, must have the versatility and flexibility to deal with military and paramilitary situations across the entire spectrum of conflict. This is a greater challenge than it may appear; conflicts of low intensity are not simply lesser forms of high-intensity war. A modern military force capable of waging a war of high intensity may find itself ill-prepared for a "small" war against a poorly equipped guerrilla force.

LEVELS OF WAR

War takes place simultaneously at several correlated levels, each with differing ends, means, characteristics, and requirements.

Activities at the *strategic* level focus directly on national policy objectives. Strategy applies to peace as well as war. Within strategy we distinguish between *national strategy*, which coordinates and focuses all the components of national power to attain the policy objective,[8] and *military strategy*, which is the application of military force to secure the policy objective.[9] Military strategy thus is subordinate to national strategy. Strategy can be thought of as the art of winning wars. Strategy establishes goals in theaters of war. It assigns forces, provides assets, and imposes conditions on the use of force. Strategy derived from national policy must be clearly understood to be the sole authoritative basis of all operations.

Activities at the *tactical* level of war focus on the application of combat power to defeat an enemy in combat at a particular time and place.[10] Tactics can be thought of as the art and science of winning engagements and battles. It includes the use of firepower and maneuver, the integration of different arms, and the immediate exploitation of success to defeat the enemy. Included within the tactical level of war is the sustainment of forces during combat. The tactical level also includes the *technical* application of combat power, which consists of those techniques and procedures for accomplishing specific tasks *within* a tactical action. These techniques and procedures deal primarily with actions designed to enhance the effects of fires or reduce the effects of enemy fires—methods such as the call for fire, techniques of fire, the technical operation of weapons and equipment, or tactical movement techniques. There is a certain overlap between tactics and techniques. We make the point only to draw the distinction between tactics, which are the product of judgment and creativity, and techniques and procedures, which are generally performed by repetitive routine.

The *operational* level of war links the strategic and tactical levels. It is the use of tactical results to attain strategic objectives.[11] The operational level includes deciding when, where, and under what conditions to engage the enemy in battle—and when, where, and under what conditions to *refuse* battle—with reference to higher aims. Actions at this level imply a broader dimension of time and space than do tactics. As strategy deals with wars and tactics with battles and engagements, the operational level of war is the art of winning campaigns. Its means are tactical results, and its end is the military strategic objective.

OFFENSE AND DEFENSE

Regardless of its type and nature or the level at which it is fought, combat manifests itself in two different but complementary forms: the offense and the defense. The offense and defense are neither mutually exclusive nor clearly distinct; as we will see, each includes elements of the other.

The offense contributes *striking power*. The offense generally has as its aim some positive gain; it is through the offense that we seek to impose some design on the enemy. The defense, on the other hand, contributes *resisting power*, the ability to preserve and protect oneself. Thus, the defense generally has a negative aim, that of resisting the enemy's will.

The defense is inherently the stronger form of combat.

Were this not the case, there would be no reason ever to assume the defensive. The offense, with its positive aim, would always be preferable.[12] But in fact, if we are weaker than our enemy, we assume the defensive to compensate for our weakness. Similarly, if we are to mount an offensive to impose our will, we must develop enough force to overcome the inherent superiority of the enemy's defense.

At least one party to a conflict must have an offensive intention, for without the desire to impose upon the other there would be no conflict. Similarly, the second party must at least possess a defensive desire, for without the willingness to resist there again would be no conflict. We can imagine a conflict in which both parties possess an offensive intention. But after the initial clash one of them must assume a defensive posture out of weakness until able to resume the offensive.

This leads us to the conclusion that while the defense is the stronger form of combat, the offense is the preferred form, for only through the offense can we truly pursue a positive aim. We resort to the defensive when weakness compels.

While opposing forms, the offense and defense are not mutually exclusive. In fact, they cannot exist separately. For example, the defense cannot be purely passive resistance. An effective defense must assume an offensive character, striking at the enemy at the moment of his greatest vulnerability. It is "not a simple shield, but a shield made up of well-directed blows."[13] The truly decisive element of the defense is the counterattack. Thus, the offense is an integral component of the concept of the defense.

Similarly, the defense is an essential component of the offense.[14] The offense cannot sustain itself indefinitely. At some times and places, it becomes necessary to halt the offense to replenish, and the defense automatically takes over. Furthermore, the requirement to concentrate forces at the focus of effort for the offense often necessitates assuming the defensive elsewhere. Therefore, out of necessity we must include defensive considerations as part of our concept of the offense.

This brings us to the concept of the *culminating point*,[15] without which our understanding of the relationship between the offense and defense would be incomplete. Not only can the offense not sustain itself indefinitely, it generally grows weaker as it advances. Certain moral factors, such as morale or boldness, may increase with a successful attack, but these generally cannot compensate for the physical losses involved in sustaining an advance in the face of resistance. We advance at a cost—lives, fuel, ammunition, physical and sometimes moral strength—and so the attack becomes weaker over time. Eventually, the superiority that allowed us to attack and forced our enemy to defend in the first place dissipates and the balance tips in favor of our enemy. We have reached the culminating point, at which we can no longer sustain the attack and must revert to the defense. It is precisely at this point that the defensive element of the offense is most vulnerable to the offensive element of the defense, the counterattack.

This relationship between offense and defense exists simultaneously at the various levels of war. For example, we may employ a tactical defense as part of an offensive campaign, availing ourselves of the advantages of the defense tactically while pursuing an operational offensive aim.

We conclude that there exists no clear division between the offense and defense. Our theory of war should not attempt to impose one artificially. The offense and defense exist simultaneously as necessary components of each other, and the transition from one to the other is fluid and continuous.

STYLES OF WARFARE

Just as there are two basic forms of combat, there are two essential components: fire and movement. Of all the countless activities in combat, we can distill them to these.

It would seem in theory that fire and movement represent opposite ends of a spectrum. But in reality, one cannot exist without the other, for fire and movement are complementary and mutually dependent. It is movement that allows us to bring our fires to bear on the enemy just as it is the protection of fires that allows us to move in the face of the enemy. It is through movement that we exploit the effects of fires while it is the destructive force of fires that adds menace to our movements.

Although all warfare uses both fire and movement, these components provide the foundation for two distinct styles of warfare: an *attrition* style, based on firepower, and a *maneuver* style, based on movement. The different styles can exist simultaneously at different levels. For example, the island-hopping campaign in the Pacific during the Second World War was a maneuver campaign comprising a series of attrition battles.

Warfare by attrition seeks victory through the cumulative destruction of the enemy's material assets by superior firepower and technology. An attritionist sees the enemy as targets to be engaged and destroyed systematically. Thus, the focus is on efficiency, leading to a methodical, almost scientific, approach to war. With the emphasis on the efficient application of massed, accurate fires, movement tends to be ponderous and tempo relatively unimportant. The attritionist gauges progress in quantitative terms: battle damage assessments, "body counts," and terrain captured. He seeks battle under any and all conditions, pitting strength against strength to exact the greatest toll from his enemy. Results are generally proportionate to efforts; greater expenditures net greater results—that is, greater attrition. The desire for volume and accuracy of fire tends to lead toward centralized control, just as the emphasis on efficiency tends to lead to an inward focus on procedures and techniques. Success through attrition demands the willingness and ability also to withstand attrition, because warfare by attrition is costly. The greatest necessity for success is numerical superiority, and at the national level war becomes as much an industrial as a military problem. Victory does not depend so much on military competence as on sheer superiority of numbers in men and equipment.

In contrast, warfare by maneuver stems from a desire to circumvent a problem and attack it from a position of advantage rather than meet it straight on. The goal is the application of strength against selected enemy weakness. By definition, maneuver relies on speed and surprise, for without either we cannot concentrate strength against enemy weakness. Tempo is itself a weapon—often the most important. The need for speed in turn requires decentralized control. While attrition operates principally in the physical realm of war, the results of maneuver are both physical and moral. The object of maneuver is not so much to destroy physically as it is to shatter the enemy's cohesion, organization, command, and psychological balance. Successful maneuver depends on the ability to identify and exploit enemy weakness, not simply on the expenditure of superior might. To win by maneuver, we cannot substitute numbers for skill. Maneuver thus makes a greater demand on military judgment. Potential success by maneuver—unlike attrition—is often disproportionate to the effort made. But for exactly the same reasons, maneuver incompetently applied carries with it a greater chance for catastrophic failure, while attrition is inherently less risky.

Because we have long enjoyed vast numerical and technological superiority, the United States has traditionally waged war by attrition. However, Marine Corps doctrine today is based on warfare by maneuver, as we will see in the fourth chapter, "The Conduct of War."[16]

COMBAT POWER

Combat power is the total destructive force we can bring to bear on our enemy at a given time.[17] Some factors in combat power are quite tangible and easily measured, such as superior numbers, which Clausewitz called "the most common element in victory."[18] Some may be less easily measured, such as the effects of maneuver, tempo, or surprise; the advantages established by geography or climate; the relative strengths of the offense and defense; or the relative merits of striking the enemy in the front, flanks, or rear. And some may be wholly intangible, such as morale, fighting spirit, perseverance, or the effects of leadership.

It is not our intent to try to list or categorize all the various components of combat power, to index their relative values, or to describe their combinations and variations; each combination is unique and temporary. Nor is it even desirable to be able to do so, since this would lead us to a formulistic approach to war.

CONCENTRATION AND SPEED

Of all the consistent patterns we can discern in war, there are two concepts of such significance and universality that we can advance them as principles: *concentration* and *speed*.[19]

Concentration is the convergence of effort in time and space. It is the means by which we develop superiority at the decisive time and place. Concentration does not apply only to combat forces. It applies equally to all available resources: fires, aviation, the intelligence effort, logistics, and all other forms of combat support and combat service support. Similarly, concentration does not apply only to the conduct of war, but also to the preparation for war.

Effective concentration may achieve decisive local superiority for a numerically inferior force. The willingness to concentrate at the decisive place and time necessitates strict economy and the acceptance of risk elsewhere and at other times. To devote means to unnecessary efforts or excessive means to necessary secondary efforts violates the principle of concentration and is counterproductive to the true objective.

Since war is fluid and opportunities fleeting, concentration applies to time as well as to space. We must concentrate not only at the decisive location, but also at the decisive moment. Furthermore, physical concentration— massing—makes us vulnerable to enemy fires, necessitating dispersion. Thus, a pattern develops: disperse, concentrate, disperse again.

Speed is rapidity of action. Like concentration, speed applies to both time and space. And, like concentration, it is *relative* speed that matters. Speed over time is tempo —the consistent ability to operate fast.[20] Speed over distance, or space, is velocity—the ability to move fast. Both forms are genuine sources of combat power. In other words, *speed is a weapon*. Superior speed allows us to seize the initiative and dictate the terms of combat, forcing the enemy to react to us. Speed provides security. It is a prerequisite for maneuver and for surprise. Moreover, speed is necessary in order to concentrate superior strength at the decisive time and place.

Since it is relative speed that matters, it follows that we should take all measures to improve our own tempo and velocity while degrading our enemy's. However, experience shows that we cannot sustain a high rate of velocity or tempo indefinitely. As a result, another pattern develops: fast, slow, fast again. A competitive rhythm develops in combat, with each belligerent trying to generate speed when it is to his advantage.

The combination of concentration and speed is momentum.[21] Momentum generates impetus. It adds "punch" or "shock effect" to our actions. It follows that we should strike the decisive blow with the greatest possible combination of concentration and speed.

SURPRISE AND BOLDNESS

We must now acknowledge two additional considerations that are significant as multipliers of combat power: *surprise* and *boldness*.

By surprise we mean striking the enemy at a time or place or in a manner for which he is unprepared. It is not essential that we take the enemy unaware, but only that he become aware too late to react effectively. The desire for surprise is "more or less basic to all operations, for without it superiority at the decisive point is hardly conceivable."[22] But, while a necessary condition for superiority, surprise is also a genuine multiplier of strength in its own right because of its psychological effect. Surprise can decisively affect the outcome of combat far beyond the physical means at hand.

Surprise is the paralysis, if only partial and temporary, of the enemy's ability to resist.[23] The advantage gained by surprise depends on the degree of surprise and the enemy's ability to adjust and recover. Surprise is based on speed, secrecy, and deception. It means doing the unexpected thing, which in turn normally means doing the more difficult thing in hopes that the enemy will not expect it. In fact, this is the genesis of maneuver—to circumvent the enemy's strength to strike him where he is not prepared. Purposely choosing the more difficult course because it is less expected necessarily means sacrificing efficiency to some degree. The question is: Does the anticipated advantage gained compensate for the certain loss of efficiency that must be incurred?[24]

While the element of surprise is often of decisive importance, we must realize that it is difficult to achieve and easy to lose. Its advantages are only temporary and must be quickly exploited. Friction, a dominant attribute of war, is the constant enemy of surprise. We must also recognize that while surprise is always desirable, the ability to achieve it does not depend solely on our own efforts. It depends at least as much on our enemy's susceptibility to surprise—his expectations and preparedness. Our ability to achieve surprise thus rests on our ability to appreciate and then dislocate our enemy's expectations. Therefore, while surprise can be decisive, it is a mistake to depend on it alone for the margin of victory.

Boldness is a multiplier of combat power in much the same way that surprise is, for "in what other field of human activity is boldness more at home than in war?"[25] Boldness "must be granted a certain power over and above successful calculations involving space, time, and magnitude of forces, for wherever it is superior, it will take advantage of its opponent's weakness. In other words, it is a genuinely creative force."[26] Boldness is superior to timidity in every instance and is at a disadvantage only in the face of nervy, calculating patience which allows the enemy to commit himself irrevocably before striking—a form of boldness in its own right. Boldness must be tempered with judgment lest it border on recklessness. But this does not diminish its significance.

Exploiting Vulnerability and Opportunity

It is not enough simply to generate superior combat power. We can easily conceive of superior combat power dissipated over several unrelated efforts or concentrated on some indecisive object. To win, we must concentrate combat power toward a decisive aim.[27]

We obviously stand a better chance of success by concentrating strength against enemy weakness rather than against strength. So we seek to strike the enemy where, when, and how he is most vulnerable. This means that we should generally avoid his front, where his attention is focused and he is strongest, and seek out his flanks and rear, where he does not expect us and where we can also cause the greatest psychological damage. We should also strike at that moment in time when he is most vulnerable.

Of all the vulnerabilities we might choose to exploit,

some are more critical to the enemy than others. It follows that the most effective way to defeat our enemy is to destroy that which is most critical to him. We should focus our efforts on the one thing which, if eliminated, will do the most decisive damage to his ability to resist us. By taking this from him we defeat him outright or at least weaken him severely.

Therefore, we should focus our efforts against a *critical enemy vulnerability*. Obviously, the more critical and vulnerable, the better.[28] But this is by no means an easy decision, since the most critical object may not be the most vulnerable. In selecting an aim, we thus recognize the need for sound military judgment to compare the degree of criticality with the degree of vulnerability and to balance both against our own capabilities. Reduced to its simplest terms, *we should strike our enemy where and when we can hurt him most*.

This concept applies equally to the conflict as a whole —the war—and to any episode of the war—any campaign, battle, or engagement. From this we can conclude that the concept applies equally to the strategic, operational, and tactical levels. At the highest level a critical vulnerability is likely to be some intangible condition, such as popular opinion or a shaky alliance between two countries, although it may also be some essential war resource or a key city. At the lower levels a critical vulnerability is more likely to take on a physical nature, such as an exposed flank, a chokepoint along the enemy's line of operations, a logistics dump, a gap in enemy dispositions, or even the weak side armor of a tank.

In reality, our enemy's most critical vulnerability will rarely be obvious, particularly at the lower levels. We may have to adopt the tactic of exploiting any and all vulnerabilities until we uncover a decisive opportunity.

This leads us to a corollary thought: exploiting opportunity. Decisive results in war are rarely the direct result of an initial, deliberate action. Rather, the initial action creates the conditions for subsequent actions which develop from it. As the opposing wills interact, they create various, fleeting opportunities for either foe. Such opportunities are often born of the disorder that is natural in war. They may be the result of our own actions, enemy mistakes, or even chance. By exploiting opportunities, we create in increasing numbers more opportunities for exploitation. It is often the ability and the willingness to ruthlessly exploit these opportunities that generate decisive results. The ability to take advantage of opportunity is a function of speed, flexibility, boldness, and initiative.

CONCLUSION

The theory of war we have described will provide the foundation for the discussion of the conduct of war in the final chapter. The warfighting doctrine which we derive from our theory is one based on maneuver. This represents a change since, with a few notable exceptions—Stonewall Jackson in the Valley, Patton in Europe, MacArthur at Inchon—the American way of war traditionally has been one of attrition. This style of warfare generally has worked for us because, with our allies, we have enjoyed vast numerical and technological superiority. But we can no longer presume such a luxury. In fact, an expeditionary force in particular must be prepared to win quickly, with minimal casualties and limited external support, against a physically superior foe. This requirement mandates a doctrine of maneuver warfare.

CHAPTER 3

Preparing for War

"The essential thing is action. Action has three stages: the decision born of thought, the order or preparation for execution, and the execution itself. All three stages are governed by the will. The will is rooted in character, and for the man of action character is of more critical importance than intellect. Intellect without will is worthless, will without intellect is dangerous."[1]

—Hans von Seekt

"The best form of welfare for the troops is first-class training, for this saves unnecessary casualties."[2]

—Erwin Rommel

"Untutored courage [is] useless in the face of educated bullets."[3]

—George S. Patton, Jr.

*D*uring times of peace the most important task of any military is to prepare for war. As the nation's rapid-response force, the Marine Corps must maintain itself ready for immediate employment in any clime and place *and in any type of conflict. All peacetime activities should focus on achieving combat readiness. This implies a high level of training, flexibility in organization and equipment, qualified professional leadership, and a cohesive doctrine.*

PLANNING

Planning plays as important a role in the preparation for war as in the conduct of war. The key to any plan is a clearly defined objective, in this case a required level of readiness. We must identify that level of readiness and plan a campaign to reach it. A campaign is a progressive sequence of attainable goals to gain the objective within a specified time.[4]

The plan must focus all the efforts of the peacetime Marine Corps, including training, education, doctrine, organization, and equipment acquisition. Unity of effort is as important during the preparation for war as it is during the conduct of war. This systematic process of identifying the objective and planning a course to gain it applies to all levels.

ORGANIZATION

The Fleet Marine Forces must be organized to provide forward-deployed or rapidly-deployable forces capable of mounting expeditionary operations in any environment. This means that, in addition to maintaining their unique amphibious capability, the Fleet Marine Forces must maintain a capability to deploy by whatever means is appropriate to the situation.

The active Fleet Marine Forces must be capable of responding immediately to most types of conflict. Missions in sustained high-intensity warfare will require augmentation from the Reserve establishment.

For operations and training, Fleet Marine Forces—active and Reserve—will be formed into Marine Air-Ground Task Forces (MAGTFs). MAGTFs are task organizations consisting of ground, aviation, combat service support, and command components. They have no standard structure, but rather are constituted as appropriate for the specific situation. The MAGTF provides a single commander the optimum combined-arms force for the situation he faces. As the situation changes, it may of course be necessary to restructure the MAGTF.

To the greatest extent practicable, Fleet Marine Forces must be organized for warfighting and then adapted for peacetime rather than vice versa. Tables of organization of Fleet Marine Force units should reflect the two central requirements of *deployability* and *the ability to task-organize according to specific situations*. Units should be organized according to type only to the extent dictated by training, administrative, and logistic requirements. Further, we should streamline our headquarters organizations and staffs to eliminate bureaucratic delays in order to add tempo.

Commanders should establish habitual relationships between supported and supporting units to develop operational familiarity among those units. This does not preclude nonstandard relationships when required by the situation.

DOCTRINE

Doctrine is a teaching advanced as the fundamental beliefs of the Marine Corps on the subject of war, from its nature and theory to its preparation and conduct.[5] Doctrine establishes a particular way of thinking about war and a way of fighting, a philosophy for leading Marines in combat, a mandate for professionalism, and a common language. In short, it establishes the way we practice our profession. In this manner, doctrine provides the basis for harmonious actions and mutual understanding.

Marine Corps doctrine is made official by the Commandant and is established in this manual. Our doctrine does not consist of procedures to be applied in specific situations so much as it establishes general guidance that requires judgment in application. Therefore, while authoritative, doctrine is not prescriptive.

LEADERSHIP

Marine Corps doctrine demands professional competence among its leaders. *As military professionals charged with the defense of the nation, Marine leaders must be true experts in the conduct of war.* They must be men of action and of intellect both, skilled at "getting things done" while at the same time conversant in the military art. Resolute and self-reliant in their decisions, they must also be energetic and insistent in execution.[6]

The military profession is a thinking profession. Officers particularly are expected to be students of the art and science of war at all levels—tactical, operational, and strategic—with a solid foundation in military theory and a knowledge of military history and the timeless lessons to be gained from it.

Leaders must have a strong sense of the great responsibility of their office; the resources they will expend in war are human lives.

The Marine Corps' style of warfare requires intelligent leaders with a penchant for boldness and initiative down to the lowest levels. Boldness is an essential moral trait in a leader, for it generates combat power beyond the physical means at hand. Initiative, the willingness to act on one's own judgment, is a prerequisite for boldness. These traits carried to excess can lead to rashness, but we must realize that errors by junior leaders stemming from over-boldness are a necessary part of learning. We should deal with such errors leniently; there must be no "zero defects" mentality.[7] Not only must we not stifle boldness or initiative, we must continue to encourage both traits *in spite of mistakes*. On the other hand, we should deal severely with errors of inaction or timidity. We will not accept lack of orders as justification for inaction; it is each Marine's *duty* to take initiative as the situation demands.

Consequently, trust is an essential trait among leaders —trust by seniors in the abilities of their subordinates and by juniors in the competence and support of their seniors. Trust must be earned, and actions which undermine trust must meet with strict censure. Trust is a product of confidence and familiarity. Confidence among comrades results from demonstrated professional skill. Familiarity results from shared experience and a common professional philosophy.

Relations among all leaders—from corporal to general —should be based on honesty and frankness, regardless of disparity between grades. Until a commander has reached and stated a decision, each subordinate should consider it his duty to provide his honest, professional opinion— even though it may be in disagreement with his senior's. However, once the decision has been reached, the junior then must support it as if it were his own. Seniors must encourage candor among subordinates and must not hide behind their rank insignia. Ready compliance for the purpose of personal advancement—the behavior of "yesmen"—will not be tolerated.

TRAINING

The purpose of all training is to develop forces that can win in combat. Training is the key to combat effectiveness and therefore is the focus of effort of a peacetime military. However, training should not stop with the commencement of war; training must continue during war to adapt to the lessons of combat.

All officers and enlisted Marines undergo similar entry-level training which is, in effect, a socialization process. This training provides all Marines a common experience, a proud heritage, a set of values, and a common bond of comradeship. It is the essential first step in the making of a Marine.

Basic individual skills are an essential foundation for

combat effectiveness and must receive heavy emphasis. All Marines, regardless of occupational specialty, will be trained in basic combat skills. At the same time, unit skills are extremely important. They are not simply an accumulation of individual skills; adequacy in individual skills does not automatically mean unit skills are satisfactory.

Commanders at each echelon must allot subordinates sufficient time and freedom to conduct the training necessary to achieve proficiency at their levels. They must ensure that higher-level demands do not deny subordinates adequate opportunities for autonomous training and that oversupervision does not prevent subordinate commanders from training their units as they believe appropriate.

In order to develop initiative among junior leaders, the conduct of training—like combat—should be decentralized. Senior commanders influence training by establishing goals and standards, communicating the intent of training, and establishing a focus of effort for training. As a rule, they should refrain from dictating how the training will be accomplished.

Training programs should reflect practical, challenging, and progressive goals beginning with individual and small-unit skills and culminating in a fully combined-arms MAGTF. In general, the organization for combat should also be the organization for training. That is, units —including MAGTFs—should train with the full complement of assigned, reinforcing, and supporting forces they require in combat.

Collective training consists of drills and exercises. Drills are a form of small-unit training which stress proficiency by progressive repetition of tasks. Drills are an effective method for developing standardized techniques and procedures that must be performed repeatedly without variation to ensure speed and coordination, such as gun drill or immediate actions. In contrast, exercises are designed to train units and individuals in tactics under simulated combat conditions. Exercises should approximate the conditions of battle as much as possible; that is, they should introduce friction in the form of uncertainty, stress, disorder, and opposing wills. This last characteristic is most important; only in opposed, free-play exercises can we practice the art of war. Dictated or "canned" scenarios eliminate the element of independent, opposing wills that is the essence of combat.

Critiques are an important part of training because critical self-analysis, even after success, is essential to improvement. Their purpose is to draw out the lessons of training. As a result, we should conduct critiques immediately after completing the training, before the memory of the events has faded. Critiques should be held in an atmosphere of open and frank dialogue in which all hands are encouraged to contribute. We learn as much from mistakes as from things done well, so we must be willing to admit and discuss them. Of course, a subordinate's willingness to admit mistakes depends on the commander's willingness to tolerate them. Because we recognize that no two situations in war are the same, our critiques should focus not so much on the actions we took as on why we took those actions and why they brought the results they did.

PROFESSIONAL MILITARY EDUCATION

Professional military education is designed to develop creative, thinking leaders. A leader's career, from the initial stages of leadership training, should be viewed as a continuous, progressive process of development. At each stage of his career, he should be preparing for the subsequent stage.

Whether he is an officer or enlisted, the early stages of a leader's career are, in effect, his apprenticeship. While receiving a foundation in professional theory and concepts that will serve him throughout his career, the leader focuses on understanding the requirements and learning and applying the procedures and techniques associated with his field. This is when he learns his trade as an aviator, infantryman, artilleryman, or logistician. As he progresses, the leader should have mastered the requirements of his apprenticeship and should understand the interrelationship of the techniques and procedures within his field. His goal is to become an expert in the tactical level of war.

As an officer continues to develop, he should understand the interrelationship between his field and all the other fields within the Marine Corps. He should be an expert in tactics and techniques and should understand amphibious warfare and combined arms. He should be studying the operational level of war. At the senior levels he should be fully capable of articulating, applying, and integrating MAGTF warfighting capabilities in a joint and combined environment and should be an expert in the art of war at all levels.

The responsibility for implementing professional military education in the Marine Corps is three-tiered: it resides not only with the education establishment, but also with the commander and the individual.

The education establishment consists of those schools —administered by the Marine Corps, subordinate commands, or outside agencies—established to provide formal education in the art and science of war. In all officer education particularly, schools should focus on developing a talent for military judgment, not on imparting knowledge through rote learning. Study conducted by the education establishment can neither provide complete career training for an individual nor reach all individuals. Rather, it builds upon the base provided by commanders and by individual study.

All commanders should consider the professional development of their subordinates a principal responsibility of command. Commanders should foster a personal teacher-student relationship with their subordinates. Commanders are expected to conduct a continuing professional education program for their subordinates which includes developing military judgment and decision making and teaches general professional subjects and specific technical subjects pertinent to occupational specialties. Useful tools for general professional development include supervised reading programs, map exercises, war games, battle studies, and terrain studies. *Commanders should see the development of their subordinates as a direct reflection on themselves.*

Finally, every Marine has a basic responsibility to

study the profession of arms on his own. A leader without either interest in or knowledge of the history and theory of warfare—the intellectual content of his profession—is a leader in appearance only. Self-study in the art and science of war is at least equal in importance—and should receive at least equal time—to maintaining physical condition. This is particularly true among officers; after all, an officer's principal weapon is his mind.

EQUIPPING

Equipment should be easy to operate and maintain, reliable, and interoperable with other equipment. It should require minimal specialized operator training. Further, *equipment should be designed so that its usage is consistent with established doctrine and tactics.* Primary considerations are strategic and tactical lift—the Marine Corps' reliance on Navy shipping for strategic mobility and on helicopters and vertical/short takeoff and landing aircraft for tactical mobility from ship to shore and during operations ashore.

Equipment that permits overcontrol of units in battle is in conflict with the Marine Corps' philosophy of command and is not justifiable.

In order to minimize research and development costs and fielding time, the Marine Corps will exploit existing capabilities—"off-the-shelf" technology—to the greatest extent possible.

Acquisition should be a complementary, two-way process. Especially for the long term, the process must identify combat requirements and develop equipment to satisfy these requirements. We should base these requirements on an analysis of critical enemy vulnerabilities and develop equipment specifically to exploit those vulnerabilities. At the same time, the process should not overlook existing equipment of obvious usefulness.

Equipment is useful only if it increases combat effectiveness. Any piece of equipment requires support: operator training, maintenance, power sources or fuel, and transport. The anticipated enhancement of capabilities must justify these support requirements and the employment of the equipment must take these requirements into account.

As much as possible, employment techniques and procedures should be developed concurrently with equipment to minimize delays between the fielding of the equipment and its usefulness to the operating forces. For the same reason, initial operator training should also precede equipment fielding.

We must guard against overreliance on technology. Technology can enhance the ways and means of war by improving man's ability to wage it, but technology cannot and should not attempt to eliminate man from the process of waging war. Better equipment is not the cure for all ills; doctrinal and tactical solutions to combat deficiencies must also be sought. Any advantages gained by technological advancement are only temporary, for man will always find a countermeasure, tactical or itself technological, which will lessen the impact of the technology. Additionally, we must not become so dependent on equipment that we can no longer function effectively when the equipment becomes inoperable.

CONCLUSION

There are two basic military functions: waging war and preparing for war. Any military activities that do not contribute to the conduct of a present war are justifiable only if they contribute to preparedness for a possible future one. But, clearly, we cannot afford to separate conduct and preparation. They must be intimately related because failure in preparation leads to disaster on the battlefield.

CHAPTER 4

The Conduct of War

"Now an army may be likened to water, for just as flowing water avoids the heights and hastens to the lowlands, so an army avoids strength and strikes weakness."[1]

—Sun Tzu

"Speed is the essence of war. Take advantage of the enemy's unpreparedness; travel by unexpected routes and strike him where he has taken no precautions."[2]

—Sun Tzu

"Many years ago, as a cadet hoping some day to be an officer, I was poring over the 'Principles of War,' listed in the old Field Service Regulations, when the Sergeant-Major came up to me. He surveyed me with kindly amusement. 'Don't bother your head about all them things, me lad,' he *said. 'There's only one principle of war and that's this. Hit the other fellow, as quick as you can, and as hard as you can, where it hurts him most, when he ain't lookin'!' "[3]*

—Sir William Slim

*The sole justification for the United States
Marine Corps is to secure or protect national
policy objectives by military force when peaceful
means alone cannot. How the Marine Corps pro-
poses to accomplish this mission is the product of
our understanding of the nature and the theory of
war and must be the guiding force behind our preparation for war.*

THE CHALLENGE

The challenge is to identify and adopt a concept of
warfighting consistent with our understanding of the nature and theory of war and the realities of the modern
battlefield. What exactly does this require? It requires a
concept of warfighting that will function effectively in an
uncertain, chaotic, and fluid environment—in fact, one

that will exploit these conditions to advantage. It requires a concept that, recognizing the time-competitive rhythm of war, generates and exploits superior tempo and velocity. It requires a concept that is consistently effective across the full spectrum of conflict, because we cannot attempt to change our basic doctrine from situation to situation and expect to be proficient. It requires a concept which recognizes and exploits the fleeting opportunities which naturally occur in war. It requires a concept which takes into account the moral as well as the physical forces of war, because we have already concluded that moral forces form the greater part of war. It requires a concept with which we can succeed against a numerically superior foe, because we can no longer presume a numerical advantage. And, especially in expeditionary situations in which public support for military action may be tepid and short-lived, it requires a concept with which we can win quickly against a larger foe on his home soil, with minimal casualties and limited external support.

Maneuver Warfare

The Marine Corps concept for winning under these conditions is a warfighting doctrine based on rapid, flexible, and opportunistic maneuver. But in order to fully appreciate what we mean by *maneuver* we need to clarify the term. The traditional understanding of maneuver is a spatial one; that is, we maneuver in space to gain a positional advantage.[4] However, in order to maximize the usefulness of maneuver, we must consider maneuver *in time* as well; that is, we generate a faster operational tempo than the enemy to gain a temporal advantage. It is through maneuver in *both* dimensions that an inferior force can achieve decisive superiority at the necessary time and place.

Maneuver warfare is a warfighting philosophy that seeks to shatter the enemy's cohesion through a series of rapid, violent, and unexpected actions which create a turbulent and rapidly deteriorating situation with which he cannot cope.

From this definition we see that the aim in maneuver warfare is to render the enemy incapable of resisting by shattering his moral and physical cohesion—his ability to fight as an effective, coordinated whole—rather than to destroy him physically through incremental attrition, which is generally more costly and time-consuming. Ideally, the components of his physical strength that remain are irrelevant because we have paralyzed his ability to use them effectively. Even if an outmaneuvered enemy continues to fight as individuals or small units, we can destroy the remnants with relative ease because we have eliminated his ability to fight effectively as a force.

This is not to imply that firepower is unimportant. On the contrary, the suppressive effects of firepower are essential to our ability to maneuver. Nor do we mean to imply that we will pass up the opportunity to physically destroy the enemy. We will concentrate fires and forces at decisive points to destroy enemy elements when the opportunity presents itself and when it fits our larger purposes. But the aim is not an unfocused application of firepower for the purpose of incrementally reducing the enemy's physical strength. Rather, it is the *selective* application of firepower in support of maneuver to contribute to the enemy's shock and moral disruption. The greatest value of firepower is not physical destruction—the cumulative effects of which are felt only slowly—but the moral dislocation it causes.

If the aim of maneuver warfare is to shatter the enemy's cohesion, the immediate object toward that end is to create a situation in which he cannot function. By our actions, we seek to pose menacing dilemmas in which events happen unexpectedly and faster than the enemy can keep up with them. The enemy must be made to see his situation not only as deteriorating, but deteriorating at an ever-increasing rate. The ultimate goal is panic and paralysis, an enemy who has lost the ability to resist.

Inherent in maneuver warfare is the need for speed to seize the initiative, dictate the terms of combat, and keep the enemy off balance, thereby increasing his friction. Through the use of greater tempo and velocity, we seek to establish a pace that the enemy cannot maintain so that with each action his reactions are increasingly late—until eventually he is overcome by events.

Also inherent is the need for violence, not so much as a source of physical attrition but as a source of moral dislocation. Toward this end, we concentrate strength against *critical* enemy vulnerabilities, striking quickly and boldly where, when, and how it will cause the greatest damage to our enemy's ability to fight. Once gained or found, any advantage must be pressed relentlessly and un-hesitatingly. We must be ruthlessly opportunistic, actively seeking out signs of weakness, against which we will di-rect all available combat power. And when the *decisive* opportunity arrives, we must exploit it fully and aggres-sively, committing every ounce of combat power we can muster and pushing ourselves to the limits of exhaustion.

The final weapon in our arsenal is surprise, the com-bat value of which we have already recognized. By study-ing our enemy we will attempt to appreciate his perceptions. Through deception we will try to shape his expectations. Then we will dislocate them by striking at an unexpected time and place. In order to appear unpredictable, we must avoid set rules and patterns, which inhibit imagination and initiative. In order to appear ambiguous and threatening, we should operate on axes that offer several courses of action, keeping the enemy unclear as to which we will choose.

PHILOSOPHY OF COMMAND

It is essential that our philosophy of command support the way we fight. First and foremost, *in order to generate the tempo of operations we desire and to best cope with the uncertainty, disorder, and fluidity of combat, command must be decentralized.* That is, subordinate commanders must make decisions on their own initiative, based on their understanding of their senior's intent, rather than passing information up the chain of command and waiting for the decision to be passed down. Further, a competent subordinate commander who is at the point of decision will naturally have a better appreciation for the true situation than a senior some distance removed. Individual initiative and responsibility are of paramount importance. The principal means by which we implement decentralized control is through the use of mission tactics, which we will discuss in detail later.

Second, since we have concluded that war is a human enterprise and no amount of technology can reduce the human dimension, our philosophy of command must be based on human characteristics rather than on equipment or procedures. Communications equipment and command and staff procedures can enhance our ability to command, but they must not be used to replace the human element of command. Our philosophy must not only accommodate but must exploit human traits such as boldness, initiative, personality, strength of will, and imagination.

Our philosophy of command must also exploit the human ability to communicate *implicitly*.[5] We believe that *implicit communication*—to communicate through *mutual understanding*, using a minimum of key, well-understood phrases or even *anticipating* each other's thoughts—is a faster, more effective way to communicate than through the use of detailed, explicit instructions. We develop this ability through familiarity and trust, which are based on a shared philosophy and shared experience.

This concept has several practical implications. First, we should establish long-term working relationships to develop the necessary familiarity and trust. Second, key people—"actuals"—should talk directly to one another when possible, rather than through communicators or messengers. Third, we should communicate orally when possible, because we communicate also in *how* we talk; our inflections and tone of voice. And fourth, we should communicate in person when possible, because we communicate also through our gestures and bearing.

A commander should command from well forward. This allows him to see and sense firsthand the ebb and flow of combat, to gain an intuitive appreciation for the situation which he cannot obtain from reports. It allows him to exert his personal influence at decisive points during the action. It also allows him to locate himself closer to the events that will influence the situation so that he can observe them directly and circumvent the delays and inaccuracies that result from passing information up the chain of command. Finally, we recognize the importance of personal leadership. Only by his physical presence—by demonstrating the willingness to share danger and privation—can the commander fully gain the trust and confidence of his subordinates.

We must remember that command from the front does not equate to oversupervision of subordinates.

As part of our philosophy of command we must recognize that war is inherently disorderly, uncertain, dynamic, and dominated by friction. Moreover, maneuver warfare, with its emphasis on speed and initiative, is by nature a particularly disorderly style of war. The conditions ripe for exploitation are normally also very disorderly. For commanders to try to gain certainty as a basis for actions, maintain positive control of events at all times, or shape events to fit their plans is to deny the very nature of war. We must therefore be prepared to cope—even better, to *thrive*—in an environment of chaos, uncertainty, constant change, and friction. If we can come to terms with those conditions and thereby limit their debilitating effects, we can use them as a weapon against a foe who does not cope as well.

In practical terms this means that we must not strive for certainty before we act for in so doing we will surrender the initiative and pass up opportunities. We must not try to maintain positive control over subordinates since this will necessarily slow our tempo and inhibit initiative. We must not attempt to impose precise order to the events of combat since this leads to a formulistic approach to war. And we must be prepared to adapt to changing circumstances and exploit opportunities as they arise, rather than adhering insistently to predetermined plans.

There are several points worth remembering about our command philosophy. First, while it is based on our warfighting style, this does not mean it applies only during war. We must put it into practice during the preparation for war as well. We cannot rightly expect our subordinates to exercise boldness and initiative in the field when they are accustomed to being oversupervised in the rear. Whether the mission is training, procuring equipment, administration, or police call, this philosophy should apply.

Next, our philosophy requires competent leadership at all levels. A centralized system theoretically needs only one competent person, the senior commander, since his is the sole authority. But a decentralized system requires leaders at all levels to demonstrate sound and timely judgment. As a result, initiative becomes an essential condition of competence among commanders.

Our philosophy also requires familiarity among comrades because only through a shared understanding can we develop the implicit communication necessary for unity of effort. And, perhaps most important, our philosophy demands confidence among seniors and subordinates.

SHAPING THE BATTLE

Since our goal is not just the cumulative attrition of enemy strength, it follows that we must have some scheme for how we expect to achieve victory. That is, before anything else, we must conceive our vision of how we intend to win.

The first requirement is to establish our intent; what we want to accomplish and how. Without a clearly identified intent, the necessary unity of effort is inconceivable. We must identify that *critical* enemy vulnerability which we believe will lead most directly to accomplishing our intent. Having done this, we can then determine the steps necessary to achieve our intent. That is, we must shape the battle to our advantage in terms of both time and space. Similarly, we must try to see ourselves through our enemy's eyes in order to identify our own vulnerabilities which he may attack and to anticipate how he will try to shape the battle so we can counteract him. Ideally, when the moment of engagement arrives, the issue has already been resolved: through our orchestration of the events leading up to the encounter, we have so shaped the conditions of war that the result is a matter of course. We have shaped the action decisively to our advantage.

To shape the battle, we must project our thoughts forward in time and space. This does not mean that we establish a detailed timetable of events. We have already concluded that war is inherently disorderly, and we cannot expect to shape its terms with any sort of precision. We must not become slaves to a plan. Rather, we attempt to shape the *general conditions* of war; we try to achieve a certain measure of ordered disorder. Examples include canalizing enemy movement in a desired direction, blocking or delaying enemy reinforcements so that we can fight a piecemealed enemy rather than a concentrated one, shaping enemy expectations through deception so that we can exploit those expectations, or attacking a specific enemy capability to allow us to maximize a capability of our own—such as launching a campaign to destroy his air defenses so that we can maximize the use of our own aviation. We should also try to shape events in such a way that allows us several options so that by the time the moment of encounter arrives we have not restricted ourselves to only one course of action.

The further ahead we think, the less our actual influence becomes. Therefore, the further ahead we consider, the less precision we should attempt to impose. Looking ahead thus becomes less a matter of influence and more a matter of interest. As events approach and our ability to influence them grows, we have already developed an appreciation for the situation and how we want to shape it.[6]

Also, the higher our echelon of command, the greater is our sphere of influence and the further ahead in time and space we must seek to impose our will. Senior commanders developing and pursuing military strategy look ahead weeks, months, or more, and their areas of influence and interest will encompass entire theaters. Junior commanders fighting the battles and engagements at hand are concerned with the coming hours, even minutes, and the immediate field of battle. But regardless of the spheres of influence and interest, it is essential to have some vision of the final result we want and how we intend to shape the action in time and space to achieve it.

DECISION MAKING

Decision making is essential to the conduct of war since all actions are the result of decisions—or of nondecisions.[7] If we fail to make a decision out of lack of will, we have willingly surrendered the initiative to our foe. If we consciously postpone taking action for some reason, that is a decision. Thus, as a basis for action, any decision is generally better than no decision.

Since war is a conflict between opposing wills, we cannot make decisions in a vacuum. We must make our decisions in light of the enemy's anticipated reactions and counteractions, recognizing that while we are trying to impose our will on our enemy, he is trying to do the same to us.

Whoever can make and implement his decisions consistently faster gains a tremendous, often decisive advantage. Decision making thus becomes a time-competitive process, and timeliness of decisions becomes essential to generating tempo. Timely decisions demand rapid thinking, with consideration limited to essential factors. We should spare no effort to accelerate our decision-making ability.

A military decision is not merely a mathematical computation. Decision making requires both the intuitive skill to recognize and analyze the essence of a given problem and the creative ability to devise a practical solution. This ability is the product of experience, education, intelligence, boldness, perception, and character.

We should base our decisions on *awareness* rather than on mechanical *habit*. That is, we act on a keen appreciation for the essential factors that make each situation unique instead of from conditioned response.

We must have the moral courage to make tough decisions in the face of uncertainty—and accept full responsibility for those decisions—when the natural inclination would be to postpone the decision pending more complete information. To delay action in an emergency because of incomplete information shows a lack of moral courage. We do not want to make rash decisions, but we must not squander opportunities while trying to gain more information.

We must have the moral courage to make bold decisions and accept the necessary degree of risk when the natural inclination is to choose a less ambitious tack, for "in audacity and obstinacy will be found safety."[8]

Finally, since all decisions must be made in the face of uncertainty and since every situation is unique, there is no perfect solution to any battlefield problem. Therefore, we should not agonize over one. The essence of the problem is to select a promising course of action with an acceptable degree of risk, and to do it more quickly than our foe. In this respect, "a good plan violently executed *now* is better than a perfect plan executed next week."[9]

MISSION TACTICS

Having described the object and means of maneuver warfare and its philosophy of command, we will next discuss how we put maneuver warfare into practice. First is through the use of mission tactics. Mission tactics are just as the name implies: the tactic of assigning a subordinate mission without specifying how the mission must be accomplished.[10] We leave the manner of accomplishing the mission to the subordinate, thereby allowing him the freedom—and establishing the duty—to take whatever steps he deems necessary based on the situation. The senior prescribes the method of execution only to the degree that is essential for coordination. It is this freedom for initiative that permits the high tempo of operations that we desire. Uninhibited by restrictions from above, the subordinate can adapt his actions to the changing situation. He informs his commander what he has done, but he does not wait for permission.

It is obvious that we cannot allow decentralized initiative without some means of providing unity, or focus, to the various efforts. To do so would be to dissipate our strength. We seek unity, not through imposed control, but through *harmonious* initiative and lateral coordination.

COMMANDER'S INTENT

We achieve this harmonious initiative in large part through the use of the commander's *intent*. There are two parts to a mission: the task to be accomplished and the reason, or intent.[11] The task describes the action to be taken while the intent describes the desired result of the action. Of the two, the intent is predominant. While a situation may change, making the task obsolete, the intent is more permanent and continues to guide our actions. Understanding our commander's intent allows us to exercise initiative in harmony with the commander's desires.

In order to maintain our focus on the enemy, we should try to express intent in terms of the enemy. The intent should answer the question: *What do I want to do to the enemy?* This may not be possible in all cases, but it is true in the vast majority. The intent should convey the commander's *vision*. It is not satisfactory for the intent to be "to defeat the enemy." To win is always our ultimate goal, so an intent like this conveys nothing.

From this discussion, it is obvious that a clear explanation and understanding of intent is absolutely essential to unity of effort. It should be a part of any mission. The burden of understanding falls on senior and subordinate alike. The senior must make perfectly clear the result he expects, but in such a way that does not inhibit initiative. Subordinates must have a clear understanding of what their commander is thinking. Further, they should understand the intent of the commander two levels up. In other words, a platoon commander should know the intent of his battalion commander, or a battalion commander the intent of his division commander.

FOCUS OF EFFORT

Another tool for providing unity is through the *focus of effort*. Of all the efforts going on within our command, we recognize the focus of effort as the most critical to success. All other efforts must support it. In effect, we have decided: *This is how I will achieve a decision; everything else is secondary*.

We cannot take lightly the decision of where and when to focus our efforts. Since the focus of effort represents our bid for victory, we must direct it at that object which will cause the most decisive damage to the enemy and which holds the best opportunity of success. It involves a physical and moral commitment, although not an irretrievable one. It forces us to concentrate decisive combat power just as it forces us to accept risk. Thus, we focus our effort against *critical enemy vulnerability*, exercising strict economy elsewhere.

Normally, we designate the focus of effort by assigning

one unit responsibility for accomplishing that effort. That unit becomes the representation of the focus of effort. It becomes clear to all other units in the command that they must support that unit in its efforts. Like the commander's intent, the focus of effort becomes a harmonizing force. Faced with a decision, we ask ourselves: "How can I best support the focus of effort?"

Each commander should establish a focus of effort for each mission. As the situation changes, the commander may shift the focus of effort, redirecting the weight of his combat power in the direction that offers the greatest success. In this way he exploits success; he does not reinforce failure.

SURFACES AND GAPS

Put simply, surfaces are hard spots—enemy strengths—and gaps are soft spots—enemy weaknesses. We avoid enemy strength and focus our efforts against enemy weakness, since pitting strength against weakness reduces casualties and is more likely to yield decisive results. Whenever possible, we exploit existing gaps. Failing that, we create gaps.

Gaps may in fact be physical gaps in the enemy's dispositions, but they may also be any weakness in time or space: a moment in time when the enemy is overexposed and vulnerable, a seam in an air defense umbrella, an infantry unit caught unprepared in open terrain, or a boundary between two units.

Similarly, a surface may be an actual strongpoint, or it may be any enemy strength: a moment when the enemy has just replenished and consolidated his position or an integrated air defense system.

An appreciation for surfaces and gaps requires a certain amount of judgment. What is a surface in one case may be a gap in another. For example, a forest which is a surface to an armored unit because it restricts vehicle movement can be a gap to an infantry unit which can infiltrate through it. Furthermore, we can expect the enemy to disguise his dispositions in order to lure us against a surface that appears to be a gap.[12]

Due to the fluid nature of war, gaps will rarely be permanent and will usually be fleeting. To exploit them demands flexibility and speed. We must actively seek out gaps by continuous and aggressive reconnaissance. Once we locate them, we must exploit them by funneling our forces through rapidly. For example, if our focus of effort has struck a surface but another unit has located a gap, we shift the focus of effort to the second unit and redirect our combat power in support of it. In this manner we "pull" combat power through gaps from the front rather than "pushing" it through from the rear.[13] Commanders must rely on the initiative of subordinates to locate the gaps and must have the flexibility to respond quickly to opportunities rather than following predetermined schemes.

COMBINED ARMS

In order to maximize combat power, we must use all the available resources to best advantage. To do so, we must follow a doctrine of combined arms. Combined arms is the full integration of arms in such a way that in order to counteract one, the enemy must make himself more vulnerable to another. We pose the enemy not just with a problem, but with a dilemma—a no-win situation.

We accomplish combined arms through the tactics and techniques we use at the lower levels and through task organization at higher levels. In so doing, we take advantage of the complementary characteristics of different types of units and enhance our mobility and firepower. We use each arm for missions that no other arm can perform as well; for example, we assign aviation a task that cannot be performed equally well by artillery. An example of the concept of combined arms at the very lowest level is the complementary use of the automatic weapon and grenade launcher within a fire team. We pin an enemy down with the high-volume, direct fire of the automatic weapon, making him a vulnerable target for the grenade launcher. If he moves to escape the impact of the grenades, we engage him with the automatic weapon.

We can expand the example to the MAGTF level: We use assault support to quickly concentrate superior ground forces for a breakthrough. We use artillery and close air support to support the infantry penetration, and we use deep air support to interdict enemy reinforcements. Targets which cannot be effectively suppressed by artillery are engaged by close air support. In order to defend against the infantry attack, the enemy must make himself vulnerable to the supporting arms. If he seeks cover from the supporting arms, our infantry can maneuver against him. In order to block our penetration, the enemy must reinforce quickly with his reserve. But in order to avoid our deep air support, he must stay off the roads, which means he can only move slowly. If he moves slowly, he cannot reinforce in time to prevent our breakthrough. We have put him in a dilemma.

Conclusion

We have discussed the aim and characteristics of maneuver warfare. We have discussed the philosophy of command necessary to support this style of warfare. And we have discussed some of the tactics of maneuver warfare. By this time it should be clear that maneuver warfare exists not so much in the specific methods used—we eschew formulas—but in the mind of the Marine. In this regard, maneuver warfare—like combined arms—applies equally to the Marine expeditionary force commander and the fire team leader. It applies regardless of the nature of the conflict, whether amphibious operations or sustained operations ashore, of low or high intensity, against guerrilla or mechanized foe, in desert or jungle.

Maneuver warfare is a way of thinking in and about war that should shape our every action. It is a state of mind born of a bold will, intellect, initiative, and ruthless opportunism. It is a state of mind bent on shattering the enemy morally and physically by paralyzing and confounding him, by avoiding his strength, by quickly and aggressively exploiting his vulnerabilities, and by striking him in the way that will hurt him most. In short, maneuver warfare is a philosophy for generating the greatest decisive effect against the enemy at the least possible cost to ourselves—a philosophy for "fighting smart."

Editors' Foreword

1. "An Officer's Principal Weapon Is His Mind," *Fast Company* magazine, 1100 Massachusetts Avenue, Cambridge, MA 02138, Vol. 1, No. 1, November 1993, p. 49.
2. *Warfighting*, p. 69.
3. *Warfighting*, p. 70.

The Nature of War

1. Carl von Clausewitz, *On War*, trans. and ed. M. Howard and P. Paret (Princeton, NJ: Princeton University Press, 1984) p. 119.
2. B. H. Liddell Hart, as quoted in *Encyclopedia Britannica*, 1929.
3. A. A. Vandegrift, "Battle Doctrine for Front Line Leaders," (Third Marine Division, 1944) p. 7.
4. For the definitive treatment of the nature and theory of war, see the unfinished classic, *On War*, by Clausewitz. All Marine officers should consider this book essential reading. Read the Princeton University Press edition, the best English translation available. This version also includes several valuable essays on the book and author and a useful guide to reading *On War*.
5. In the strict legal sense, the United States enters a state of

war only by formal declaration of Congress, which possesses the sole constitutional power to do so. The United States has declared war on five occasions: with Britain (1812); with Mexico (1846); with Spain (1898); with Germany and Austria-Hungary (1917); and with Japan, Germany, Italy, Bulgaria, Hungary, and Rumania (1941–2). A President, as commander in chief, may commit U.S. Forces to military action without a declaration of war when the circumstances do not warrant or permit time for such a declaration. Militarily there will be little if any distinction between war and military action short of war. Within this context, this book will focus on the military aspects of war, and the term *war* as discussed here will apply to that state of hostilities between or among nations regardless of the existence of a declaration of war.

6. Clausewitz, *On War*, p. 121.

7. For a first-hand description of human experience and reaction in war, read Guy Sajer's *The Forgotten Soldier* (Annapolis, MD: Nautical and Aviation Publishing Co., 1988), a powerful account of the author's experience as a German infantryman on the eastern front during the Second World War and ultimately a tribute to the supremacy of the human will.

8. Clausewitz: "Kind-hearted people might, of course, think there was some ingenious way to disarm or defeat an enemy without too much bloodshed, and might imagine this is the true goal of the art of war. Pleasant as it sounds, it is a fallacy that must be exposed: war is such a dangerous business that the mistakes which come from kindness are the very worst . . .

"This is how the matter must be seen. It would be futile—

even wrong—to try to shut one's eyes to what war really is from sheer distress at its brutality." *On War*, pp. 75–76.

9. For an insightful study of the reaction of men to combat, see S.L.A. Marshall's *Men Against Fire* (New York: William Morrow and Co., 1961).

10. *The American Heritage Dictionary* (New York: Dell Publishing Co., 1983).

11. In his often-quoted maxim, Napoleon assigned an actual ratio: "In war, the moral is to the material as three to one."

The Theory of War

1. Clausewitz, *On War*, p. 87.

2. Sun Tzu, *The Art Of War*, trans. S.B. Griffith (New York: Oxford University Press, 1982) p. 85. Like *On War*, *The Art of War* should be on every Marine officer's list of essential reading. Short and simple to read, *The Art of War* is every bit as valuable today as when it was written about 400 B.C.

3. Winston S. Churchill, *The World Crisis* (New York: Charles Scribner's Sons, 1923) vol. II, p. 5. The passage continues: "Nearly all battles which are regarded as masterpieces of the military art, from which have been derived the foundation of states and the fame of commanders, have been battles of manoeuvre in which the enemy has found himself defeated by some novel expedient or device, some queer, swift, unexpected thrust or stratagem. In many battles the losses of the victors have been small. There is required for the composition of a great commander not only massive common sense and

reasoning power, not only imagination, but also an element of legerdemain, an original and sinister touch, which leaves the enemy puzzled as well as beaten. It is because military leaders are credited with gifts of this order which enable them to ensure victory and save slaughter that their profession is held in such high honour . . .

"There are many kinds of manoeuvre in war, some only of which take place upon the battlefield. There are manouevres far to the flank or rear. There are manoeuvres in time, in diplomacy, in mechanics, in psychology; all of which are removed from the battlefield, but react often decisively upon it, and the object of all is to find easier ways, other than sheer slaughter, of achieving the main purpose."

4. Clausewitz, On War, p. 87. We prefer the phrase with military force rather than by military force as translated since military force does not replace the other elements of national power, but supplements them.

5. Ibid., pp. 87–88.

6. Clausewitz, On War, p. 77.

7. The National Security Strategy of the United States (Washington: The White House, 1988), pp. 7–8, lists the elements of national power as moral and economic example, military strength, economic vitality, alliance relationships, public diplomacy, security assistance, development assistance, science and technology cooperation, international organizations, and diplomatic mediation.

8. Also referred to as grand strategy or the policy level. From JCS Pub. 1-02: "National Strategy—(DOD, IADB) The art and science of developing and using the political, economic, and psychological powers of a nation, together with its

armed forces, during peace and war, to secure national objectives."

9. JCS Pub. 1-02: "**Military Strategy**—(*DOD*, *IADB*) The art and science of employing the armed forces of a nation to secure the objectives of national policy by the application of force or the threat of force."

10. JCS Pub. 1-02: "**Tactical Level of War**—(*DOD*) The level of war at which battles and engagements are planned and executed to accomplish military objectives assigned to tactical units or task forces. Activities at this level focus on the ordered arrangement and maneuver of combat elements in relation to each other and to the enemy to achieve combat objectives."

11. JCS Pub. 1-02: "**Operational Level of War**—(*DOD*) The level of war at which campaigns and major operations are planned, conducted, and sustained to accomplish strategic objectives within theaters or areas of operations. Activities at this level link tactics and strategy by establishing operational objectives needed to accomplish the strategic objectives, sequencing events to achieve the operational objectives, initiating actions, and applying resources to bring about and sustain these events. These activities imply a broader dimension of time or space than do tactics; they ensure the logistic and administrative support of tactical forces, and provide the means by which tactical successes are exploited to achieve strategic objectives."

12. Clausewitz, *On War*, pp. 84, 357–359.

13. *Ibid.*, p. 357.

14. Clausewitz argued (p. 524) that while the offense is an integral component of the concept of defense, the offense is con-

ceptually complete in itself. The introduction of the defense into the concept of the offense, he argued, is a necessary evil and not an integral component.

15. Clausewitz, *On War*, p. 528.

16. The United States Army has also adopted a doctrine based on maneuver, called "AirLand Battle." The principal doctrinal source is Field Manual 100-5, *Operations* (1986).

17. JCS Pub. 1-02: "**Combat Power**—(*DOD, NATO*) The total means of destructive and/or disruptive force which a military unit/formation can apply against the opponent at a given time."

18. Clausewitz, *On War*, p. 194.

19. *Ibid.*, p. 617.

20. Tempo is often associated with a mental process known variously as the "Decision Cycle," "OODA Loop," or "Boyd Cycle," after retired Air Force Colonel John Boyd who pioneered the concept in his lecture, "The Patterns of Conflict." Boyd identified a four-step mental process: observation, orientation, decision, and action. Boyd theorized that each party to a conflict first observes the situation. On the basis of the observation, he orients; that is, he makes an estimate of the situation. On the basis of the orientation, he makes a decision. And, finally, he implements the decision—he acts. Because his action has created a new situation, the process begins anew. Boyd argued that the party that consistently completes the cycle faster gains an advantage that increases with each cycle. His enemy's reactions become increasingly slower by comparison and therefore less effective until, finally, he is overcome by events.

21. From basic physics, momentum is the product of mass and velocity: $M = mv$.

22. Clausewitz, *On War*, p. 198.

23. Edward N. Luttwak, *Strategy: The Logic of War and Peace* (Cambridge, MA: Belknap Press of Harvard University Press, 1987) p. 8.

24. Luttwak, *Strategy: The Logic of War and Peace*, pp. 8–10.

25. Clausewitz, *On War*, p. 190.

26. *Ibid.*

27. We should note that this concept is meaningless in attrition warfare in its purest form, since the identification of critical vulnerability by definition is based on selectivity, which is a foreign thought to the attritionist. In warfare by attrition, any target is as good as any other as long as it contributes to the cumulative destruction of the enemy.

28. Sometimes known as the *center of gravity*. However, there is a danger in using this term. Introducing the term into the theory of war, Clausewitz wrote (p. 485): "A center of gravity is always found where the mass is concentrated the most densely. It presents the most effective target for a blow; furthermore, the heaviest blow is that struck by the center of gravity." Clearly, Clausewitz was advocating a climactic test of strength against strength "by daring all to win all" (p. 596). This approach is consistent with Clausewitz' historical perspective. But we have since come to prefer pitting strength against weakness. Applying the term to modern warfare, we must make it clear that by the enemy's center of gravity we do not mean a source of strength, but rather a critical vulnerability.

Preparing for War

1. Hans von Seekt, *Thoughts of a Soldier*, trans. G. Waterhouse (London: Ernest Benn Ltd., 1930) p. 123.

2. Erwin Rommel, *The Rommel Papers*, ed. B.H. Liddell Hart, trans. P. Findlay (New York: Da Capo Press, Inc., 1985) p. 226.

3. George S. Patton, Jr., *Cavalry Journal*, April 1922, p. 167.

4. JCS Pub. 1-02: "**Campaign Plan**—(*DOD, IADB*) A plan for a series of related military operations aimed to accomplish a common objective, normally within a given time and space." As defined, a campaign plan pertains to military operations, but the thought applies equally to preparations.

5. JCS Pub. 1-02: "**Doctrine**—(*DOD, IADB*) Fundamental principles by which the military forces or elements thereof guide their actions in support of national objectives. It is authoritative but requires judgment in application."

6. Field Manual 100-5, *Tentative Field Service Regulations* (Washington: Government Printing Office, 1939) p. 31.

7. Clausewitz: "In a commander a bold act may prove to be a blunder. Nevertheless it is a laudable error, not to be regarded on the same footing as others. Happy the army where ill-timed boldness occurs frequently; it is a luxuriant weed, but indicates the richness of the soil. Even foolhardiness—that is, boldness without object—is not to be despised: basically it stems from daring, which in this case has erupted with a passion unrestrained by thought. Only when boldness rebels against obedi-

ence, when it defiantly ignores an expressed command, must it be treated as a dangerous offense; then it must be prevented, not for its innate qualities, but because an order has been disobeyed, and in war obedience is of cardinal importance." *On War,* pp. 190–191.

The Conduct of War

1. Sun Tzu, *The Art of War,* p. 101.
2. *Ibid.,* p. 134.
3. Sir William Slim, *Defeat into Victory* (London: Cassell and Co. Ltd., 1956) pp. 550–551.
4. JCS Pub. 1-02: "**Maneuver**—(*DOD, NATO*) . . . 4. Employment of forces on the battlefield through movement in combination with fire, or fire potential, to achieve a position of advantage in respect to the enemy in order to accomplish the mission."
5. Boyd introduces the idea of implicit communication as a command tool in his lecture, "An Organic Design for Command and Control."
6. Hence the terms *area of influence* and *area of interest.* JCS Pub. 1-02: "**Area of Influence**—(*DOD, NATO*) A geographical area wherein a commander is directly capable of influencing operations, by maneuver or fire support systems normally under his command or control." "**Area of Interest**—(*DOD, NATO, IADB*) That area of concern to the commander, including the area of influence, areas adjacent thereto, and extending into enemy territory to the objectives of current or

planned operations. This area also includes areas occupied by enemy forces who could jeopardize the accomplishment of the mission."

7. Much of the material in this section is adapted from John F. Schmitt's article, "Observations on Decisionmaking in Battle," *Marine Corps Gazette*, March 1988, pp. 18–20.

8. Napoleon Bonaparte, "Maxims of War," *Napoleon and Modern War; His Military Maxims*, annotated C.H. Lanza (Harrisonburg, PA: Military Service Publishing Co., 1953) p. 19.

9. George S. Patton, Jr., *War As I Knew It* (New York: Houghton Mifflin, 1979) p. 354.

10. JCS Pub. 1-02: "**Mission Type Order**—(*DOD, IADB*) . . . 2. Order to a unit to perform a mission without specifying how it is to be accomplished."

11. JCS Pub. 1-02: "**Mission**—(*DOD, IADB*) 1. The task, together with the purpose, which clearly indicates the action to be taken and the reason therefor."

12. The well known Soviet *fire-sack* defense, for example.

13. Hence the terms *reconnaissance pull* and *command push* respectively. See William S. Lind's *Maneuver Warfare Handbook* (Boulder, CO: Westview Press, 1985) pp. 18–19.

U.S. GOVERNMENT PRINTING OFFICE: 1991 — 338–046